Sanara C. Baia
Izaias L. Tavares
Antonio M. J. S. Pereira

Non-verbal language on WhatsApp®

Sanara C. Baia
Izaias L. Tavares
Antonio M. J. S. Pereira

Non-verbal language on WhatsApp®

Signs, signifiers and meanings attributed to the app's emojis

ScienciaScripts

Imprint

Cover image: www.ingimage.com

This book is a translation from the original published under ISBN 978-3-330-76123-0.

Publisher:
Sciencia Scripts
is a trademark of
Dodo Books Indian Ocean Ltd. and OmniScriptum S.R.L publishing group

120 High Road, East Finchley, London, N2 9ED, United Kingdom
Str. Armeneasca 28/1, office 1, Chisinau MD-2012, Republic of Moldova, Europe
Printed at: see last page
ISBN: 978-620-8-36400-7

DEDICATORY

I dedicate this book to my beloved son Anthony Guilherme, because it was for him and for him that I remained strong and confident throughout my academic journey, so I dedicate this achievement to him, the love of my life today and always.
Sanara Correa Baia

To my children: My Chubby and My Princess, whose faces and mouths have always been my favourite Emojis. To my sweet mum, because all my work on this earth was only possible because of her efforts to keep me alive. I love you all.
Izaias Loureiro Tavares

To my son, Tomás Jacques Pereira, and my wife, Gerlany de Fátima dos Santos Pereira.
Antonio Marcos de Jesus de Souza Pereira

SUMMARY

The use of applications that connect to the internet has grown considerably. Among them is the WhatsApp® application, which in addition to various features that facilitate communication, has a keyboard on its platform that has digital signs called Emojis. The centrepiece of this work is the non-verbal language used in the application in question, through the use of Emojis. The aim was to understand how users utilise this communication tool in order to make digital text more expressive. To this end, questionnaires were administered within the Google Drive Virtual Environment, with links sent via the WhatsApp® application itself and distributed throughout the virtual network. The results of the survey showed the identification of the main meanings attributed to these Emojis in the digital discourse used by users. It's worth a look!

Keywords: Sign. WhatsApp®. Emoji.

CONTENTS

CHAPTER 1

INTRODUCTION

Given that verbal and non-verbal means of communication have been instruments of communication since the dawn of humanity. And considering that with the evolution of technology in the globalised world, virtual communication tools are occupying more and more space in people's daily lives, especially the multiplatform application WhatsApp®, this work seeks to identify the main signs, signifiers and meanings attributed to Emojis in the WhatsApp® environment. Non-verbal communication on WhatsApp® and its Emoji signs have become a salutary and pertinent discussion among people who use mobile communication technology and who are becoming increasingly dependent on this communication practice.

The topic became pertinent from the outset of the data survey, as it had been detected that communication via the WhatsApp® application is so notorious and growing within the academic environment. It brings together more and more users, with varying age groups and an increasingly realistic approach, which is also complex and subjective. The way each Emoji is placed in the conversation implies various meanings, depending on the point of view and understanding of each human being involved.

This non-verbal language, which stimulates practical communication with the use of these signs in the WhatsApp® application, is relevant to the issue under study, because with a glossary with terminology drawn up using appropriate academic methodology, the identification of the different meanings of the most commonly used signs in a WhatsApp® message conversation optimises the communication process.

We realise that non-verbal language and its signs and meanings on WhatsApp® had famous predecessors, widespread since its introduction through characters on IRC (Internet Relay Chat) and later on the now defunct Orkut, MSN and the still in use Facebook. Here, people began to use figures, illustrations, images, symbols and Emojis as a means of communication to express an idea, an emotional state, an opinion, among other things. With the arrival of WhatsApp®, the use of these linguistic codes has become more frequent, in other words, in real time people can communicate or pass on information to a large number of users, where they can interact individually (with the PV feature, or private messaging), or in groups formed according to interests, entertainment, family, work, where the spread of information through this tool has become very fast.

It's clear that real-time communication has a positive impact when it comes to the benefits that the tool has brought to its frequent users. The speed of information, the agility in resolving problems of a professional, personal and family nature, study groups, among other issues that enable resolutions of a diverse nature. Based on the assumption that non-verbal language through the meaning of Emojis on WhatsApp® is currently in continuous and reciprocal use, its benefit and objective is to improve understanding of these signs and highlight new concepts that have been contextualised and shared by users and non-users of this application throughout the research.

Thus, the general objective of this research is to identify the different meanings attributed to the signs corresponding to Emojis in the WhatsApp® environment, by understanding and dimensioning the main notions of signs and meanings within verbal and non-verbal language. And as specific objectives: the delimitation of meanings to Emojis in non-verbal communication within the WhatsApp® application and the debate within the application and its own virtual discussion spaces on the approximations and distances between the different concepts of Emojis through WhatsApp®.

These objectives were only possible due to the fact that there are several meanings within the same sign that vary according to the prior knowledge of each user of this application. And because human beings, in exercising their singularity and objectivity, attribute various meanings to the same Emoji and this can in some cases distort non-verbal communication, it is therefore necessary to universalise and unify the meaning of the Emojis in the app. Finally, it is necessary to distinguish between similar and different concepts regarding an Emoji used by a group in the app.

In this sense, the theoretical path of this research crosses the thresholds of communication and interaction, going through the origins of the communicative process and the forms of verbal and non-verbal communication, before presenting the basic theoretical foundation on linguistic signs and virtual interaction. The research then turns to the application under study as a revolution in the communication process, dissecting its characteristics and particularities until it reaches the presentation of the research materials and methods and the results obtained, the discussion of which will focus on two fronts, namely: the meanings attributed to Emojis in non-verbal communication within WhatsApp® and the approximations and differences in the different concepts attributed to WhatsApp® Emojis.

CHAPTER 2

LITERATURE REVIEW

This chapter is made up of the following items: 2.1 Communication and Interaction (2.1.1 Origins of the Communicative Process; 2.1.2 Forms of verbal and non-verbal communication; 2.1.3 Introduction to linguistic signs; 2.1.4 Application emojis) and 2.2 WhatsApp®: the instant messaging revolution (2.2.1 Features and peculiarities of the WhatsApp® application).

2.1 COMMUNICATION AND INTERACTION

When we talk about communication, we know that it is the process of exchanging information between a sender (who sends the message) and a receiver (who receives it), and the aspect that can influence this communicative process is known as the linguistic code, which in turn must be understood by both parties.

> Communication takes place through the transfer of information, under two main conditions. The first condition is the presence of two systems: a sender and a receiver; the second is the transmission of messages (CORRAZE, apud MESQUITA, 1997).

Communication occurs when two or more people interact, producing an exchange of information through the use of language, where language in turn occurs in this exchange of information between receiver and sender, also known as interlocutors, who are the parties involved in the process of interaction through the use of language.

In communication there is the code, which in turn is the set of socially adjusted signs for the elaboration and transmission of messages, which must be understood by the receiver and sender. There is also the communication channel, which is made up of physical or virtual means that promote the circulation of messages, which must guarantee that communication really takes place between sender and receiver. And the message is the object of communication as a whole, which in turn is made up of the information contained in the communication.

By using the word as a code, whether written or spoken, verbal communication is promoted, which according to Luft (1994) is characteristic of the *Homo sapiens* species, language in the true sense of the word: 'animal language' is rather a figurative use of the term. Verbal communication is still the most used in everyday life, as it is present in all forms through advertising, texts, literary works, conversations between friends and even in the form of messages via social networks.

When communication takes place by means other than verbal or written, we are dealing with non-verbal communication. "Communication can take place through gestures, knocks, whistles, colours and other signs" (LUFT, 1994). Contrary to popular belief, non-verbal communication is very important and has the power to keep the reader's attention just as much as written text. Given that this type of communication has been taking up more and more space with the emergence of social networks, where communication has been made easier through symbols and images that form socio-interactional communication.

The object of study in this book was non-verbal communication signs, more precisely WhatsApp® Emojis, which promote non-verbal communication by giving various meanings to the same linguistic sign, which in some cases can make it difficult for one of the parties involved in the communication process to understand the other.

For Saussure (2006), language is a system of signs, where the sign is the central factor of language, "the sign is equal to the signifier plus the signified". It is a combination of meaning and image, so the sign in itself already had a finalised meaning, soon after which Saussure divided the sign into two parts, the first called the meaning which refers to the concept of the sign and the second called the signifier which corresponds to the acoustic image.

Still according to Saussure (2006), language is a system of signs that express ideas, and is therefore comparable to writing, the alphabet of the deaf, symbolic rites, forms of politeness, military signs, etc., etc. To complement this, Chauí's (2000) meaning is ultimate, when he asserts that language is a system of signs or signals used to indicate things, for communication between people and for the expression of ideas, values and feelings.

The elements that make up the linguistic sign are strongly related, which is why it is said that a sign is nothing more than the relationship established between meaning and signifier. The signified is the preconceived idea of a given signifier, i.e. a concept acquired through experience, or even a concept from a dictionary.

If we insert the concept of linguistic sign into the WhatsApp® application, we can see that it mostly uses non-verbal language through the Emojis that make up the application. These Emojis, in turn, are increasingly indispensable in the app's communication environment. Given that users of the app always use Emojis in every conversation, this makes communication more dynamic and efficient.

Media communication has been revolutionised through the constant use of these resources in dialogue, since communication is not only related to speech and writing. In most cases, it is related to non-verbal language, writing and speech. This interaction takes place largely within a context of communication that is synonymous with practical communication, in a society that increasingly needs to use the minimum amount of time in communication, whether formal or informal.

Media resources have always been important for human communication. Ducrot and Todorov (1998, p. 237) state that "In the broad sense, writing is any visual semiotic system and in the narrow sense, it is a graphic system of language notation". Given this statement, Emojis can be defined in the broad sense of writing, given that they are a visual tool.

In the contemporary era, Lévy (1996, p. 15) states that "we live in a civilisation of the image" and, as mobile phones are the means of visual communication, Emojis, by simulating human expressions, are considered digital signs. Just as in face-to-face communication it is possible to perceive the bodily characteristics of the sender of the message, Emojis have the task of conveying the same emotions in distance communication as linguistic signs and in turn convey emotions, sensations and even natural phenomena.

When you talk in text, you need facial and body expressions, which in turn are necessary for understanding a message. This is why the use of Emojis has become essential at times. The non-verbal language of Emojis helps us to understand details and feelings, as the brain associates them with a human face, since the brain is adapting to a universe full of digital signs.

It can be said that one of the peculiarities of communication via the WhatsApp® application is the creativity in the use of language associated with Emojis, which in turn is necessary to make oneself understood, as stated by Zacharias (2005, p. 10):

> When we only have a written text, it's more difficult to understand what emotion the sender is expressing. If we don't have enough data in the writing itself to give us an indication, it's possible that we'll interpret the phrase
> **by giving it the 'tone of voice' we want or choose, which doesn't necessarily correspond to the writer's intention, the same sentence can be said or 'read' in an aggressive, loving, desperate way, etc.**

Even with their easy-to-understand visual characteristics, Emojis have meanings that many users don't know or understand. Just as there arc signs that have universal meaning and collective understanding, there are also those that have ambiguous meanings. In other words, several meanings for the same sign can make it difficult to understand the discourse.

As there are several signs in the app and several different expressions, the relationship of meaning with the sign varies according to each user. This is why it is necessary to limit the meaning of Emojis, which in turn also vary according to the group in which the user is inserted. This is compared to the culture of a society where a gesture can be commonplace for some and offensive for others.

Therefore, the mutual understanding of the parties involved in communication where there are media resources is essential if this process is not to fail in terms of understanding the message sent by the sender. The use of emojis can lead to a breakdown in the receiver's understanding. In view of this, we can see the dispersion in the use of non-verbal language, specifically WhatsApp® Emojis, which requires a universalised understanding.

There are two ways in which communication actually takes place: verbally and non-verbally. Verbal communication is divided into oral and written, through texts, messages, etc. Non-verbal communication, on the other hand, has been evolving and gaining greater proportions in applications such as WhatsApp® itself, where it is possible to establish communication using only images, gestures, dances and so on, which, unlike verbal language, does not use words.

This is what happens when you use Emojis in the WhatsApp® application, where you can use them to express a message, feelings and emotions. The field of linguistics can be used to study each of the meanings attributed to these Emojis, which are considered linguistic signs that carry an unbiased meaning and a signifier. A linguistic sign is anything that has a meaning and a signifier.

2.1.1 Origins of the Communicative Process

Communication has been present since the dawn of time, with what are known as "cavemen" who, looking at it from a more global perspective, must have first communicated through signs and symbols. Many years later, some began to use grunts, gestures and even shouts to express themselves. We can see that man already felt the need to communicate with his fellow human beings.

Then, thousands of years later, came the well-known cave paintings, which are nothing more than illustrated representations of life in prehistoric times. They depicted a form of communication through drawings made on the walls and ceilings of caves where primitive people lived. In order to demonstrate what they experienced and knew, they created a kind of "uncivilised daily representation" that today serves as a starting point for studies into the ancestry of human communication.

> Primitive art is a legacy of inscriptions and rocks that has defied time, surviving for thousands of years and still transmitting information about a non-existent civilisation even after the emergence of writing as a milestone in history (GOMES, 2007, p. 03).

Even with cave paintings that managed to convey certain ideas through drawings, this means of communication was still not enough for man to express himself. It was then, around 4000 BC, that the Sumerians in Mesopotamia developed the first manifestation of cuneiform writing, which was based on clay tablets. Meanwhile, in Egypt, writing was also being developed which was divided into two forms, demotic and hieroglyphic, where one was less elaborate and the other much more elaborate respectively.

> The Egyptian writing system almost entirely reproduced spoken language, as some of its pictograms already represented syllables. In addition to pictograms, it was made up of phonograms (representation of sounds) and other decisive signs. In that civilisation, writing is closely linked to the recording of sacred rituals, harvests, seasons and the movement of the Nile. From its phonograms, we can say that Egyptian writing already constituted a more or less approximate idea of an alphabet, as it already had a characteristic of syllabic representations (GOMES, 2007 p. 7-8).

In spite of everything, Sumerian writing was made up of symbols that had only one meaning and this only allowed for a very vague reading. So, in 800 BC, the Greeks took a very important step in writing, separating vowels from consonants and finally arriving at the complete alphabet, as shown in the image below:

IMAGE 01: Cuneiform writing.

SOURCE: https://i.ytimg.com/vi/iXeEJYJ-oLw/maxresdefault.jpg

Once they had a language and writing, they needed a support to spread it. In the middle of 105 AD, paper was first produced by Cai Lun in China from bamboo, until it was introduced in Japan in 610. This art was peculiar to China and was only introduced in Egypt in the year 800. In the middle of the 15th century, malleable paper was created, making it easier to print books.

It was 1438 when the German blacksmith Gutenberg developed the Gutenberg press, which revolutionised the printing of documents and made writing more popular and accessible to everyone. He gained even more prestige in 1456 when he printed the Bible, which to this day is the most printed and sold book in the world, and from this invention there was a great reduction in the cost of producing books, thus allowing greater access. During this period, the main means of communication were letters, newspapers and books.

In 1837 Samuel Morse made the first transmissions using a device called the telegraph, which consisted of transmitting codes using electricity. From the telegraph came the telephone, which is also a telecommunications device that allows sounds to be transmitted using electrical signals. Developed for a restricted audience, the first domestic handsets appeared in the 1890s, and became popularly known as the "iron foot". From then on, the telephone developed as new technologies emerged, until it reached today's mobile phones.

In 1940, a means of communication emerged that became so popular that it became known as the mass medium: radio revolutionised the world in that decade. Years later, in 1895, the Lumière brothers created the cinematograph, which consisted of recording images. It was very versatile as it allowed films to be recorded and projected. Driven by the invention of the cinematograph, television was born. Television broadcasting began in 1936 in England, still in black and white, and developed even further after the Second World War.

In mid-1943 the first computer was created, called ENIAC (Electronic Numeral Integrator and Computer), the brainchild of professors John Mauchly and J. Presper-Eckert, who proposed the construction of this device to the US army during the Second World War, with the aim of helping with precision calculations.

With the computer came the internet in 1969 in the US. Initially called ARPAnet, it belonged exclusively to the US defence department and linked research laboratories. It was only in 1987 that the Internet ceased to be restricted to the scientific environment and was released for commercial use. Today, the Internet has become the main means of communication linked to electronic devices that make it possible to send and receive messages instantaneously.

The process of exchanging information via the Internet gained authenticity with the creation of the system for sending and receiving instant messages, as it was a medium that allowed individuals from different parts of the world to exchange messages in real time. Users establish virtual interaction and use technological resources to expand their thinking. This reinforces McLuhan's theory of the global village, which suggests that individuals are no longer exclusively influenced by their social group of origin, as they have been since the primates.

However, it had countless references as influences, in order to create a group of affinities with different citizens and customs, thus breaking down physical barriers. The forerunner in the process of instant communication via Internet messaging was ICQ (a chat programme), which was soon replaced by MSN (Messenger). The nature of both was to provide greater interaction through short texts using the Internet. When applied to personal communication, the method was conceptualised as leisure.

Mobile devices have expanded communication alternatives beyond conventional orality, bringing together countless applications in just one instrument, the mobile phone. SMS allowed users to send messages with a maximum of 180 characters, while MMS allowed messages with a higher number of characters, also making it possible to send multimedia content such as audio, images and videos. The spread of the internet has created bolder devices for users who need to connect at all times.

The experiment in the area of more affectionate and obvious interaction changed the idea of iconic communication, as all the resources available on the device were identified using icons. The symbols used for identification became so popular in the technological environment that they also became part of communication in environments other than just the virtual one.

2.1.2 Verbal and non-verbal forms of communication

Communication used to be understood as the act of sharing, expressing, exposing ideas, feelings or thoughts, making information common, so the act of communicating is a basic human need. For Corraze (1982), human communication takes place through the transfer of information, under two main conditions. The first condition is the presence of two systems, namely: a sender and a receiver: the second is the transmission of messages.

For communication to take place in any medium, there must always be a sender and receiver, where the communicative process takes place through the exchange of information by both parties. Communication goes beyond the simple exchange of messages between sender and receiver, it encompasses the external aspects that make it up. In this respect, Alcure (1996) states that communication is not only done with words. Gestures, touch, visual and audio images, even olfactory and gustatory sensations are part of the resources available for communication. Like words, the senses also adapt the human being to the socio-environmental environment, constituting sources of knowledge (ALCURE, 1996).

Human life and behaviour are governed by information, persuasion, words, sounds, colours, shapes, gestures, facial expressions and symbols. Understanding is no longer only done through spoken or written language, but also through radio, television, newspapers, music, cinema and advertising in all media (SOARES, 1999). It is therefore understood that language takes place through other means and not just through written or even spoken words.

For this reason, the focus of this book is on non-verbal language and how it occurs in the WhatsApp® application. Non-verbal language is all communication that takes place without the use of written or spoken words. It only uses gestures, drawings, facial and body expressions, paintings or through the object of study of this work: the Emojis belonging to the WhatsApp® application, which through a simple representation manage to convey emotions, states and other situations.

According to Corraze (1982), human non-verbal communication takes place through three media. The first is the body, in its physical and physiological qualities and movements. The second is the human body, i.e. objects associated with the body such as ornaments, clothing or even mutilations, marks or scars from tattoos, rituals or otherwise; this medium also includes the products of human skill that can be used for communication. Finally, the third support refers to the dispersion of individuals in space, this space encompasses everything from the physical space that surrounds the body to the space that relates to it, the territorial space.

Faced with this issue, it is clear that in personal verbal communication there are indicators that make it easier to understand the message, such as body movement, voice intonation, glances, gestures, etc. and it is noticeable that these signals contribute significantly to personal communication. Therefore, there was a need to also express these signals in interpersonal communication, where non-verbal language can become predominant through the Emojis of the WhatsApp® application, given that in distance communication these non-verbal elements are impossible to perceive. Thus, to fulfil this need in distance communication, Emojis are an essential tool, helping to understand the message.

2.1.3Introduction to linguistic signs

Saussure (2006, p.80), the linguist who coined the term "linguistic sign", defines it as "uniting not only a thing and a word, but a concept and an acoustic image". From this we can see that the sign is a psychic entity made up of two sides: the acoustic image (sound) and the concept (idea), which can also be called the signifier and the signified respectively.

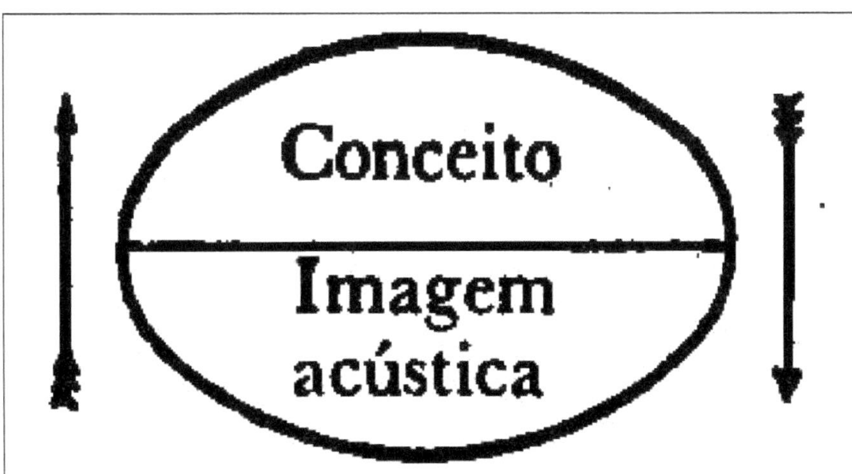

IMAGE 02: Sassure's concept of linguistics.

SOURCE: SAUSSURE, 2006, p. 80

This image shows that the concept is to the acoustic image as the acoustic image is to the concept, where one depends on the other. The signifier corresponds to the acoustic image, i.e. the relationship between the sound and the letters, but it doesn't make complete sense if there is no concept of the signifier. For example, when you teach a child a word while they are still developing their vocabulary, they are not yet able to relate the word to the image, so if there is no contact or experience with the image that the sound represents, it is not possible to establish the relationship between meaning and signifier.

> The linguistic sign transmits (or conveys) information using a material and perceptible part associated with an immaterial and intelligible part. The sensible part is the signifier and the non-sensible part is the signified (BORBA, 1998, p. 19).

Based on this precept, it can be said that a given concept is always subject to an image and vice versa. Understanding and dimensioning the main notions of signs and meanings within verbal and non-verbal language. Whose representation with the absence of the sound of speech is replaced by its own sign of the image of language. Delimiting meanings to Emojis in non-verbal communication within the application.

Signs are only representative for those who are part of the culture to which the symbols belong and which can change according to cultures. Thus, what represents something to one person may not represent anything to another (GOMDIM, 2012 apud MADUREIRA; SOUZA, 2015).

Attributing the concept of linguistic sign to the Emojis of the WhatsApp® application, it can be said that each Emoji is a sign, where an Emoji has a signifier and a signified, thus making it a sign.

2.1.4 Application emojis

Considering that Emojis are signs and are frequently used by users of the WhatsApp® application, they have visual characteristics similar to the human face and its facial expressions or can even indicate some action or natural phenomenon. It can be said that Emoji are the embodiment of non-verbal communication, because a message can be expressed through a single sign. Thus:

> They are Japanese icons used in the virtual world, mainly on smartphones, in chats and emails to represent faces, weather, vehicles, buildings, celebrations, food and drink, feelings and activities, in other words, they serve as a tool to expand communication. The word Emojis is the translation of a pictogram meaning e = image + mó = writing + ji = character written through images (MADUREIRA; SOUZA, 2015, p. 9).

It should be emphasised that when communicating via instant messaging, some artifice is needed to define and improve the decoding of the message. This is because virtual communication lacks the resources that exist in face-to-face communication, such as gestures, facial expressions and even the tone of the voice, as can be seen in the image below:

IMAGE 03: First WhatsApp® Emoji Base.

SOURCE: http://blogdetec.blogfolha.uol.com.br

It is therefore worth discussing the origins of Emojis, the frequency with which they are encountered and the reasons for their inclusion in digital discourse, since long before the digital age took over the world, these representations were already used to represent emotions through written text. Initially known as smileys, these faces were used in SMS when today's well-known emojis did not yet exist. They were created in 1982 as a way of expressing what you wanted to say through written text. From then on, people began to create new Smileys using only the characters on their keyboard.

Over time, these faces have been refined into the current Emoji, which appeared in Japan in the mid-1990s and are actually an improvement on the old Smiley or Emoticon. Emojis have ended up forming part of multimodal discourse, as they can be found through the WhatsApp® application and integrated into discourse, thus providing the recipient with a better understanding of the message, using both text and images, because

> [...] the use of images makes digital text more interesting and less tiring. They are important not only for navigating programmes and communicating between people of different languages, and some can be characterised as universal symbols, such as a piece of pizza. According to the author, icons are effective tools for keeping a conversation interesting, since the construction of meaning is done simultaneously by both parties (MADUREIRA; SOUZA, 2015, p. 9).

Emojis are therefore imagery resources capable of promoting communication with complete meaning, if both parties, receiver and sender, understand the sign in the same way. However, they do not replace oral or written communication, which already has ready-made content. Emojis are not only a new non-verbal digital communication tool, they are also signs loaded with affection, as Brito (2008, p. 5) states:

> They are able to express the feelings of interlocutors who are physically distant from each other. Therefore, the emotions

> experienced by computer users don't cease to exist because they are being mediated by machines, they just take on a different format and circulate in a different way, because with virtualisation, there has been a need to create new ways of expressing affection and language.

Finally, Lévy (1988, p. 15) corroborates the above assertion when he says that "we live in a civilisation of the image". And since mobile phones are the means of visual communication, Emojis, by simulating human expressions, are considered digital signs, capable of conveying the same emotions in long-distance communication as linguistic signs. The same author addresses the issue of hypermedia and multicodes within the framework of the concept of Virtualisation, which is based on theories linked to verbal language, including the textualist and deconstructionist strands, which are no longer suitable for this analysis, considering the current technological scenario.

2.2 WHATSAPP®: THE INSTANT MESSAGING REVOLUTION

Today's society is characterised by an exacerbated increase in access to information in a short space of time, linked to the means of communication that produce this rapid communication and circulation of information quickly and efficiently. Today the mobile phone is much more than a mobile phone. It is configured as a "teletudo", a device that is at the same time a telephone, camera, television, cinema, receiver of journalistic information, e-mail and SMS broadcaster, WAP5, website updater (moblogs), GPS, music player (MP3 and other formats), electronic wallet, etc. (LEMOS; VALENTIM, 2006).

The media and the technologies that emerge every day are more present in people's lives, and a large part of their daily activities are devoted to communicating through these new technologies, which are growing enormously. The impact of these changes is so great that many observers have concluded that we are currently living in an information society (STRAUBHAAR; LARROSE, 2004).

Every culture is transformed according to the information technology introduced into it. Technology can be defined as the use of scientific knowledge to define the means capable of changing something subject to reproduction.

> Of course, technology does not determine society. Nor does society write the course of technological transformation, since many factors, including creativity and entrepreneurial initiative, intervene in the process of scientific discovery, technological innovation and social applications, so that the final result depends on a complex interactive pattern (CASTELLS, 2005, p. 43).

Instant messaging, as the applications that make it possible to exchange information via Information Technology (IT) can be called. They have changed over the years and transformed the lives of their users since the 1990s, when instant messaging began using mobile phones.

Relatively recently, the history of the Internet has seen various means of making communication quick and easy. And before these communicators, users didn't have any method of doing so. Then came the well-known IRC (Instant Relay Chat) protocol, which was one of the forerunners of today's communicators. It made it possible to exchange messages in chat rooms or private rooms, so it fell out of favour in the mid-2000s with the emergence of other more robust and powerful instant communicators.

With the demise of IRC came ICQ (image 04), which lasted on the internet until the mid-2000s. It was the 'gateway' to Internet applications for beginners, as it made it possible to send messages and even files. It soon fell into disuse, losing ground to the new instant messaging apps that were growing rapidly and evolving in every aspect.

IMAGE 04: mIRC and ICQ chat screens

SOURCE: http://www.techtudo.com.br

Then came Windows Live Messenger (image 05), or as it is popularly known, MSN. It's the most popular instant messaging software from Microsoft®, and has been at the top of the most used communication methods for a long time. Over the years it has been modified and updated to keep it in use.

IMAGE 05: MSN chat screen

SOURCE: http://www.techtudo.com.br

Between the rise and fall of various communicators, Facebook emerged (image 06). As well as communicating and posting on the user's wall or profile, it also allows private messages to be exchanged in an in-app chat. In addition to sharing images, location, audio and other devices.

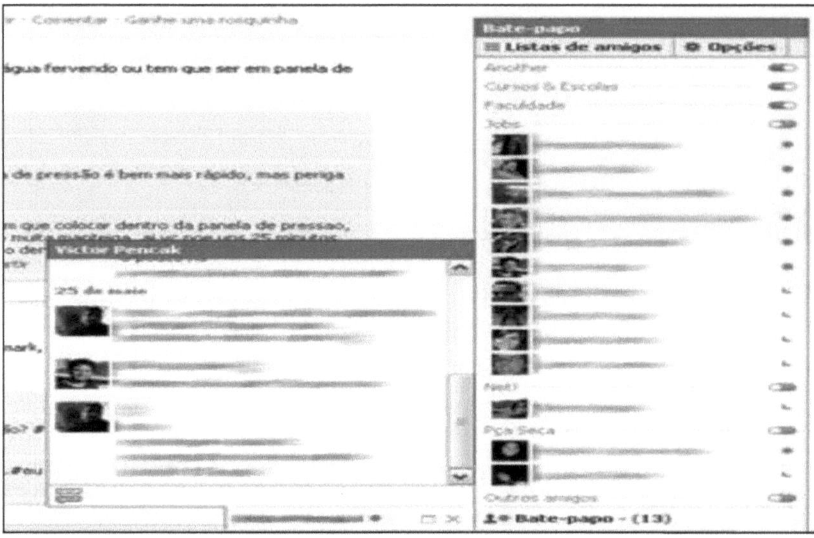

IMAGE 06: Facebook chat screen

SOURCE: http://www.techtudo.com.br

And finally we've reached the top of the instant messaging charts. The most popular and widely used today is the WhatsApp® application (image 07), which is described on its official website as:

> A multi-platform messaging app that lets you exchange messages on your mobile phone (...) There's no cost to send messages and stay in touch with your friends. In addition to basic messages, WhatsApp® users can create groups, send (...) images, videos, location, contacts and audio."[1]

Created in 2009 by Brian Actor and Jam Koum, both of whom worked together at Yahoo, it is considered to be the world's most popular instant messaging service with

[1] http://www.whatsapp.com

a presence in more than 100 countries and has over 250 million active users.

IMAGE 07: WhatsApp® logo

SOURCE: WhatsApp®.com

In 2014, the app was bought by Facebook, making it even more popular and competing directly with Twitter, which has over 200 million users.

2.2.1Features and peculiarities of the Whatsapp® application

The WhatsApp® application is compatible with Android, IOS, Windows Phone and BlackBerry devices. It can be installed free of charge via the Play Store, the virtual smartphone shop, for users of the Android® operating system.

Once you've downloaded WhatsApp®, installation is simple: you'll have to enter your phone number and enter a code received via SMS to validate your mobile phone and line. The application then synchronises your contacts and anyone who has WhatsApp® is automatically transferred to a tab on the right of your smartphone screen. You can also send an invitation to contacts who don't yet have the application installed

Once the application has been installed, it can be used to send and receive messages in the same way as SMS messages, with the only criterion being the use of an active mobile data network, be it Wi-Fi, 3G or 4G. This allows messages to be exchanged using text, images, audio, etc., as well as group chats with a maximum of 256 members.

Since its inception, the WhatsApp® application has undergone a number of improvements. Initially, only text messages were allowed. Then, with an update in 2013, it became possible to send audios using voice commands, saving users a significant amount of time. This update also brought the possibility of sharing images, locations, videos and other types of files.

The app's page on the Play Store announces new features in the 2015 update. These include the possibility of making calls via the app, using the internet connection, as well as the facility to mark messages, making it easier to locate them later. WhatsApp® also has confirmation ticks, where one tick indicates that the message has been sent, two ticks indicate that the message has been delivered and when the tick turns blue, it indicates that the message has been read by the recipient (image 08).

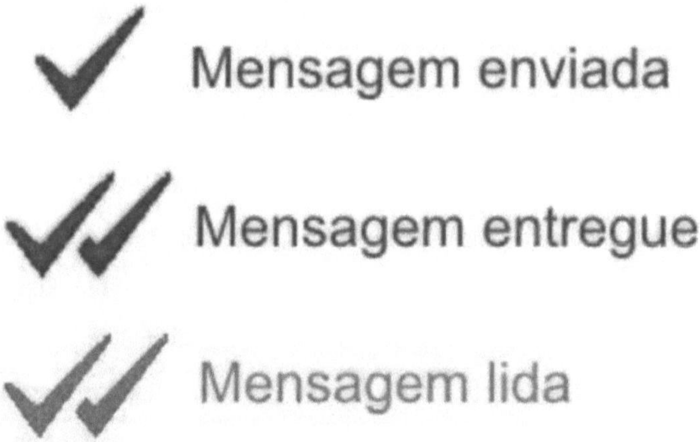

IMAGE 08: Delivery Notifications/Application Reading
SOURCE: www.queromaisdicas.com.br430 x 233

These and other attributes have made the WhatsApp® application an indispensable means of communication, given the convenience and practicality it offers. It is considered to be the best instant communicator today and combines the successful features of various instant communication platforms that have already been created. As a result, it is becoming more and more accepted as a communication tool, and more and more users are connecting to it. WhatsApp® is the ideal research environment, as analysed in all the items discussed so far.

CHAPTER 3

MATERIALS AND METHODS

The research was explanatory, where the researcher will explain the causes and relationships that guide non-verbal language, as well as the meanings given to the Emojis of the WhatsApp® application, thus correlating the similarities and differences of each meaning.

This was an indirect research approach, as it used ready-made data obtained by analysing data obtained through closed questionnaires posted on the internet so that users of the WhatsApp® application on social networks could collaborate to reach a conclusion on each meaning attributed to the main Emojis in the application.

The methodological option of the research was comparative, as it seeks to understand through comparisons the different meanings attributed to the main Emojis of the WhatsApp® application by the research subjects and making a relationship between similar and non-similar meanings regarding the object in question.

The tools used in this research were an open online questionnaire using the Google Docs tool, which collected randomised data on the different meanings attributed to the same sign.

The particularity of similar and divergent responses was taken into account, thus concluding the concept that users have of a bell in common. The data collection technique for this research consisted of an open-ended questionnaire.

The area worked on included the responses to the form published on the WhatsApp® application, where data was collected through questionnaires applied to users of the application, prioritising the similarities of the responses obtained and thus analysing the relationship that WhatsApp® users make with each linguistic sign.

After publicising the link for collecting data from the responses (https://goo.gl/ynvpRD), which was created using a link shortener called Google URL

Shortener[2] , the form was accessed more than 600 times (image 09) in various parts of the world, with the highest number of hits per day occurring in February, as can be seen in the image below:

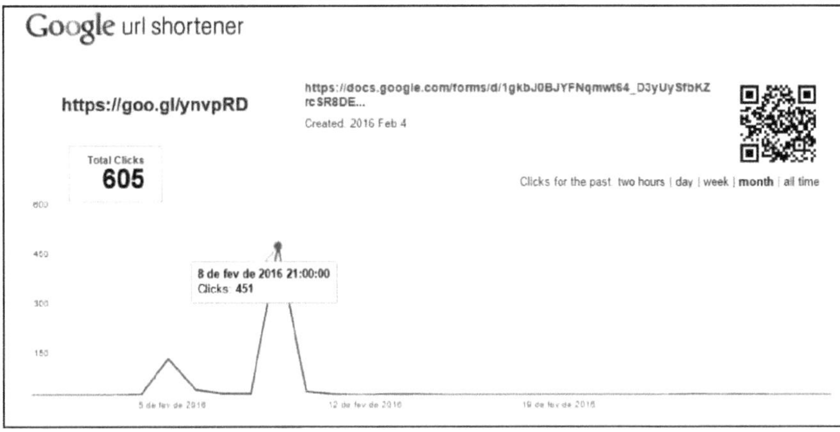

IMAGE 09: General Data for Accessing the Electronic Form

SOURCE: Field Research - Computerised System

It was also found that the survey was answered with greater voracity 754 when the link to the electronic form was shared on the social network Facebook® (image 10), meaning that more than 53 per cent of the responses received came from that platform and it was also possible to confirm that 76 per cent of respondents were users of the Google Chrome® browser, both for computers and mobile phones.

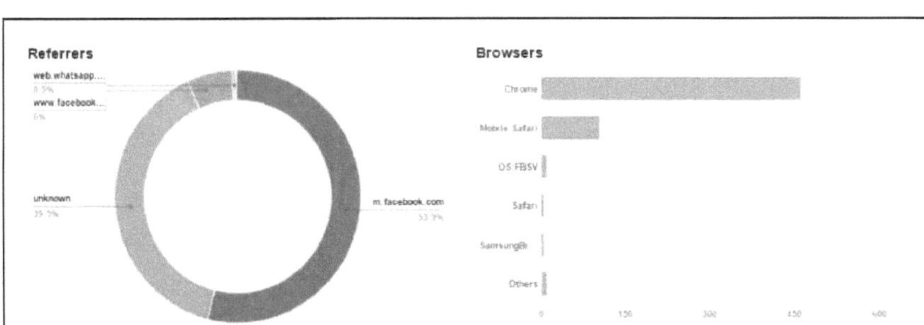

IMAGE 10: General Data on Fonts and Browsers Used

[2] http://goo.gl

SOURCE: Field Research - Computerised System

The survey also reached a global scale, with respondents in Spain and India accessing and filling in the electronic form, and there was also a predominance of the Android operating system over other research platforms, as 89.58 per cent of accesses to the electronic form-filling environment were via devices with this system (image 11).

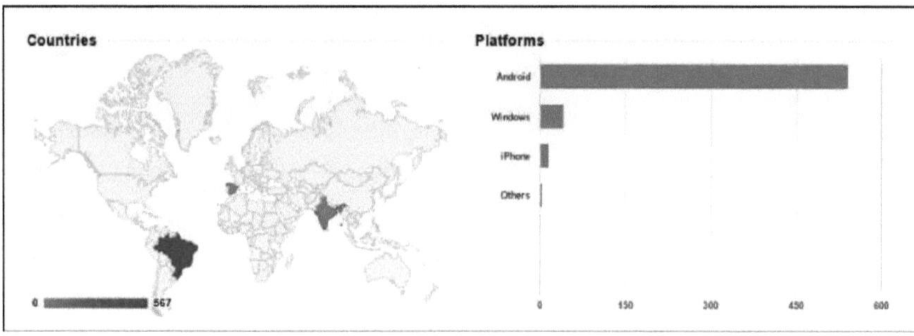

IMAGE 11: General Access Data by Country and Operating Systems

SOURCE: Field Research - Computerised System

Finally, when accessing the computerised system for filling in the answers, the researchers took care to insert the Online Free and Informed Consent Form (TECLEO) so that the respondents could fill in the form.

Of the 275 raw responses received, a different behaviour of the respondents was observed which directly affects the results received. By characterising the profile of the survey participants in order to support subsequent analyses, we were able to see how young the survey participants were and how much time they spent using Emojis in the app for both personal and professional academic purposes. The answers that make these inferences possible are described in graphs 01 to 03, as follows:

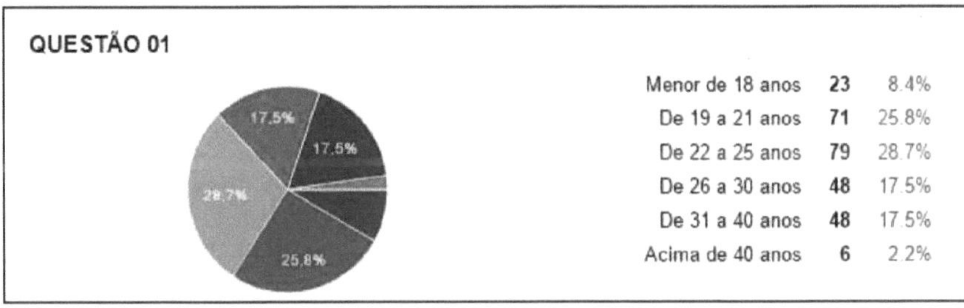

GRAPH 01: Age distribution of survey participants

SOURCE: Field Research - Computerised System

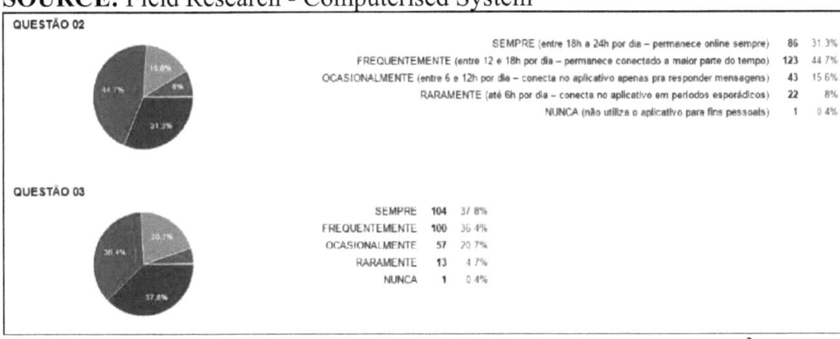

CHART 02: Time Spent and Use of Emojis in Personal Conversations[3]

SOURCE: Field Research - Computerised System

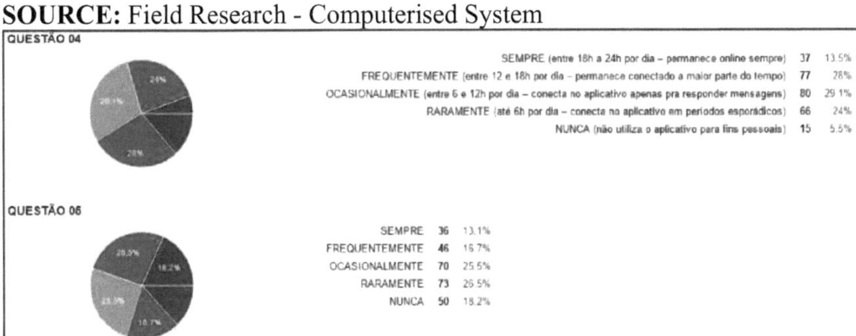

GRAPH 03: Time Spent and Use of Emojis in Academic/Professional Conversations[4]

---

[3] QUESTION 02 - Approximately how much time a day do you use the WhatsApp® application for personal purposes?
QUESTION 03 - How often do you use Emojis in the WhatsApp® application during personal conversations?

[4] QUESTION 04 - Approximately how much time a day do you use the WhatsApp® application during academic and/or professional conversations?

SOURCE: Field Research - Computerised System

Given the scenario presented, it is very important to characterise that, in the universe surveyed randomly through an electronic form, 54% of the responses received were from young people aged 19 to 25. Who are frequently online on the app, between 12 and 18 hours a day - remaining connected for most of the time available for personal conversations - (44.7%). Who always or often (74.8%) use Emojis for these conversations.

In the same vein, this same group fluctuates in their availability for academic and professional conversations, being rarely, occasionally and often available (71.1%), which means that they remain online from 6 to 18 hours a day, where more than 50% use Emojis in this type of communication rarely or occasionally.

This statement provides the necessary information to be able to analyse the results obtained with a better understanding of the cause, as follows.

QUESTION 05 - How often do you use Emojis on WhatsApp® during professional or academic conversations?

CHAPTER 4

RESULTS AND DISCUSSIONS

In view of the results obtained through the questionnaire, the main data and answers obtained through computerised data collection are presented below. With the information from the respondents associating the differences and similarities in the meanings of the Emojis used in this research.

4.1 SMILING FACE WITH SMILING EYES

IMAGE 12: Smiling Face Emoji with Smiling Eyes

SOURCE: http://emojipedia.org/grinning-face-with-smiling-eyes/

A version of the smiley face, which looks more closely like a face that grimaces. Due to the popularity of Emoji, it's commonly used as a face making faces, rather than a (smiley) face with smiling eyes.

Image 12 is officially called *"Grmnigg Face With Smiling Eyes",* which roughly translates as "smiling face with smiling eyes". To this question, 26 of the 201 answers to this question resemble the use of Emoji with this connotation. Here are the main differences:

Chart 01: Main divergent responses to the "Grinning Face With Smiling Eyes" Emoji:

Fear
Apparatus doll
A smile to apologise
Fighting with the person
Irony

Source: Field research

Regarding the variations in meanings found for the same Emoji, Madureira (2015) states that the varied meanings found for the icons are a consequence of the situation and the culture, each specimen has a meaning and tells a story in its own right. Feelings such as fear and irony, shown in table 01, illustrate the situation pointed out by the author, where in the context of virtual communication, the Emoji reflects these feelings on its own, even if for other users the meaning varies for the same Emoji.

4.2 FACE SENDING A KISS

IMAGE 13: Smiling Face Emoji with Smiling Eyes

SOURCE: http://emojipedia.org/face-throwing-a-kiss/

The image shows a face sending a kiss. One eye is open, the other is blinking. A heart is shown coming out of the mouth. The Emoji illustrated in image 13 officially stands for "Face *Throwing a Kiss",* or "face sending a kiss". Where 50 out of 147 answers to this question come close to the real meaning of the Emoji. The table below shows the main deviant answers.

Chart 02: Deviant responses to the "Face *Throwing a Kiss"* Emoji:

In love
Faith
Kiss on the heart
Mess
Miss you

Source: Field research

The same Emoji can have different meanings depending on the context of the conversation in which it is inserted. In this case, the "Face *Throwing a Kiss"* Emoji had very different variations. Martino (apud MADUREIRA; SOUZA, 2015) states that the meaning of the sign is given from the code or reference in which it is inserted. A sign can have several meanings depending on the environment against which it is contrasted. This explains the divergence of meanings regarding the same Emoji, even though the sign is universal.

4.3 SMILING FACE WITH HEART-SHAPED EYES

PICTURE 14: Smiling face with heart-shaped eyes

SOURCE: http://emojipedia.org/smiling-face-with-heart-shaped-eyes/

A face with hearts instead of eyes. It is generally used as an expression of love, for example: "I love you" or "I love this". Image 14 shows the Emoji "Smi/ing *Face With Heart-Shaped EyeS* or commonly known as "smiling face with heart-shaped eyes". There were 136 answers to this question, 57 of which had the same meaning as the original. The main different answers are listed below.

Chart 03: Main distinct responses to the *"Smiling Face With Heart-Shaped Eyes" Emoji*:

When I get a compliment or statement
When people send me photos I like or when they compliment me
Beautiful
Beautiful things vary a lot, because everyone interprets them in different ways.
Caring

Source: Field research.

According to chart 03, the use of Emoji brings an informality to virtual communication, making dialogue more interactive and with a certain affectivity present in the discourse, as Brito (2008, p. 2) states:

> [...] they are digital image signs often used in chats [...] to express feelings. In addition, they are seen by Internet users as an uncomplicated, informal, playful and consequently more attractive alternative for communicative interaction.

It can be seen that the illustrated Emoji obtained different responses, but with the same level of interpretation, always perceiving the affectivity present in the sign.

4.4 SLEEPY FACE

IMAGE 15: Sleepy Face

SOURCE: http://emojipedia.org/sleepy-face/

This sleepy face emoji features a snot bubble coming out of the nose. This is used in anime and manga to indicate that a character is asleep. Officially called *"Sleyyy Face",* image 15 illustrates the Emoji popularly known as "sleepy face". 184 responses were collected for this Emoji, of which only 6 were close to the real meaning of the image. The table below lists the main divergent answers.

Table 04: List of the main distinct responses to the "Sleepy **Face"** Emoji:

Runny nose
Sad and wanting to cry
Boredom
Discontent
Tiredness

Source: Field research.

An Emoji can be applied depending on the context of the dialogue, at any moment of virtual communication, with the particularity of not having linearity. In other words, at any moment, at the beginning or end of the discourse, it will be used with its meaning. With regard to the linearity of emojis, Storto (2011) states that one of their characteristics is precisely that they are not linear.

its non-linear, non-sequential nature, with no beginning or end, often compared to associative thought processes.

The answers in table 04 show the linearity of the sign, where it can be used at any moment in the conversation and always maintain its meaning, or the meaning used for it.

4.5 . CRYING FACE

IMAGE 16: Crying face

SOURCE: http://emojipedia.org/crying-face/

A sad face with a single tear running from one eye down the cheek. Hurt and upset, but not crying hysterically. The Emoji shown in image 16 is officially known as "Crying *Face",* and popularly referred to as "crying face". There were 141 answers to this question, of which 57 were the same as the meaning of the Emoji. The table below lists the main divergent cases.

Chart 05: Main divergent responses to the **"Crying Face" Emoji**:

Horrified
Thrilled
Scared
Apprehensive
I use it when I feel stressed

Source: Field research.

The association of Emojis with human emotions or expressions means that the user becomes familiar with the sign and applies its own meaning or variant according to the context of the conversation. Answers obtained for the Emoji *cCryigg Face"* denote a feeling of emotion on the part of the user, such as "thrilled" or "apprehensive", even though they don't have the real meaning of the Emoji, they still carry human expressiveness in their meaning.

Regarding the predominance of the characteristics of human expressiveness for a sign, Madureira and Souza (2015) emphasise that icons must have predominant characteristics so that they can be associated with the human expressions corresponding to their indices. This expressiveness present in the sign facilitates understanding and comprehension of a particular Emoji.

4.6 THOUGHTFUL FACE

IMAGE 17: Thoughtful Face

SOURCE: http://emojipedia.org/pensive-face/

A repentant and thoughtful face. Saddened by life. Quietly considering where things went wrong. The Emoji represented in image 17 is called "Pensive *Face"* or "thoughtful face" in popular knowledge.

A total of 119 answers were collected for this question, of which only 57 had the same meaning as the original one. The table below highlights the answers that differed in meaning.

Chart 06: Different responses to the "Pensive Face" Emoji:

Scared
Desolate
Enfatuado
Tired
Needy

Source: Field research

The Emoji represented in image 16 apparently has a universal meaning, so each user may have a different interpretation of the same sign. As can be seen in table 06, it is still possible to see divergent responses to the same Emoji. In this respect, Madureira and Souza (2015) state that the meaning attributed to Emoji icons, despite some seemingly obvious meanings, is subjective. Each individual can interpret the icons differently.

4.7 FATIGUED FACE

IMAGE 18: Tired face

SOURCE: http://emojipedia.org/weary-face/

A troubled face, with an open mouth and crescent-shaped eyes. It seems to have given up on life. Very similar in appearance to the Weary Face Emoji. The Emoji shown in the image above is called "Weary Face" and can easily be confused with the tired face Emoji. 43 of the 201 responses collected resemble the use of the Emoji in this sense. Below are the main differences.

Chart 07: Main dissimilar responses to the use of the "Weary Face" Emoji:

Screaming with tears
Complaining
Nervous
Anguish
Worried

Source: Field research.

Contrary to popular belief, Emojis are not simply a conversational device, as Storto (2011, p. 20) demonstrates:

> [...] they are not mere drawings placed in digital conversations to decorate them, but, contrary to what one might think, they are loaded with meaning, significance, endowed with argumentative power, and can cause the most diverse effects of meanings in the texts in which they are inserted.

So you can see that a single Emoji within a simple sentence can make the meaning of the text change or have a totally different tone than it would if it were absent. In the different responses to the "Weary *Face"* Emoji, such as "screaming with tears" or "anguish", you can see the load of meaning that the Emoji brings to the dialogue, even if it's not the same as the literal meaning of the sign.

4.7 THUMB UP

PICTURE 19: Raised thumb

SOURCE: http://emojipedia.org/thumbs-up-sign/

A gesture of a raised thumb indicating approval. The image above shows the very popular Emoji"*tr hUumSs Up Sign"*, commonly known as the "thumbs up". A total of 132 resolutions were reached on this question, of which 123 stated that they use the Emoji in this way. Below is a list of the divergences found.

Chart 08: Selected divergent answers for the "Thumbs **Up Sign" Emoji**:

The story is over
I'm watching
I don't want to prolong the subject
Anger
Fuck off

Source: Field research.

Even though there are countless variations in the meaning of the same Emoji, it should be understood that they are predefined concepts that vary according to the context in which they are used. Storto (2011, p. 21) demonstrates that Emoji:

> [...] it is not a prop for virtual conversations, but a new form of linguistic manifestation, in which the reader interacts with the text, as they make associative links, relating the image to pre-established codes between the interlocutors.

4. 9 EYES

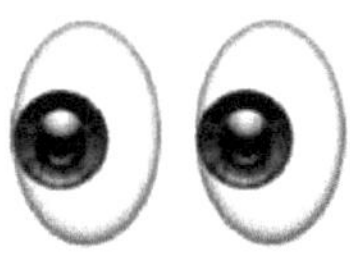

IMAGE 20: Eyes
SOURCE: http://emojipedia.org/eyes/

A pair of eyes, looking slightly sideways. Sometimes used to indicate perverted eyes to indicate approval of an attractive photo posted online or "naughty eyes" to show that you are doing or observing something deceitful.

A controversial sign is represented in image 20, called "Eyes" or simply "eyes", this Emoji is very popular among users of the WhatsApp® application. There were 125 responses to this question, 55 of which defined the Emoji as having a similar meaning to the original. Among the divergent answers, the following are highlighted in the table below.

Chart 09: Main divergent answers about the "Eyes" Emoji:

When I'm surprised by something
Keeping an eye on you
Mistrust/scared
Connected to the chat
When I don't want to say anything, I just want to show that I'm watching.

Source: Field research

The contextualisation of the meaning created for an Emoji comes from culture. Variation also depends on the context in which it is found, which is why the difference in meaning for a single sign in question is so striking. Thus, signs do not exist outside of social relations, they are neither outside of time nor outside of history.

Thought and language are linked to the space in which they were produced, they are not autonomous systems of meaning as if they had come "out of nowhere". The motherhood of the sign lies in its links with the society in which it originates. Signs follow the dynamics of society, but there is nothing automatic about the process (MARTINO, 2010).

4.10 FACE SCREAMING WITH FEAR

IMAGE 21: Face Screaming with Fear

SOURCE: http://emojipedia.org/face-screaming-in-fear/

A screaming face with both hands holding its jaw and cheeks in fear. The wide eyes are shown with an open mouth. Shown in image 20 is the Emoji called "Face *Screaming in Fear*", or popularly known as "face screaming in fear". In this question, 97 answers were in favour of the formal meaning of the Emoji, the main different answers are listed below.

Chart 10: Main different answers regarding the meaning of the Emoji *'Fcee Screaming in* Fear*':*

When I get scared about something.
Surprised
Great fright
Ashamed
Absurd

Source: Field research.

According to Madureira and Souza (2015), the sign has different social applications that provide different experiences, from caves to the Emojis used in virtual communication. This means that the variation that exists for the same sign is inevitable and has existed since the beginning. Faced with answers such as "Ashamed" or "Absurd", we can realise that different answers like these come from different types of experiences and different understandings.

4.11ROSTO CORADO

IMAGE 21: Blushing face

SOURCE: http://emojipedia.org/flushed-face/

An embarrassed face with blushing red cheeks. This face is blushing because of a mistake or other embarrassing situation. Image 21 is officially called *"Flushed Face'* which more popularly means "blushing face". A total of 159 resolutions were found for this question, 56 of which are similar to the original meaning of the sign. The main divergences are listed in the table below.

Table 11: List of the main divergences in the answers to the sign *FFluhhdd Face'"* or "Blushing Face":

When I get scared about something
Strange conversations
WHAT?
Surprised / disappointed
Incredulous

Source: Field research.

Answers such as "Surprised/disappointed" and "Incredulous", despite being distinct from the real meaning of the sign in image 21, can never be considered incorrect, given that Emojis have characteristics that resemble the human face, yet they can be interpreted in a variety of ways, thus facilitating communication and making it more practical.

And in the absence of resources used almost involuntarily in personal communication, Emojis fill this gap in virtual communication. Emojis thus help electronic interaction to be similar to oral language, reducing the absence of other conversational features [such as intonation].

4. 12SMILING FACE WITH SUNGLASSES

IMAGE 22: Smiling face with sunglasses

SOURCE: http://emojipedia.org/smiling-face-with-sunglasses/

A smiling face wearing sunglasses, which is used to denote a feeling of cold. The sluggish Emoji has a similar face, but with normal prescription glasses. The Emoji represented in image 22 is called "SmzVzng *Face With Sunglasses",* but commonly referred to as "smiley face with sunglasses". Of the 193 answers obtained to this question, 21 were close to the real meaning attributed to the Emoji. The main differences are highlighted in the table below.

Chart 12: Dissimilar answers **to the question about the sign** *"Smiligg Face With Sunglasses"*:

Feeling great
Taking a wave
Quiet, beautiful, I'm the best
Over the dry cam
It's quiet, it's favourable

Source: Field research.

Much more than a communicative device, Emojis carry a great deal of significance within a discourse, as Storto argues that

> [...] not only do they decorate writing, giving it affectivity, which in itself would be an addition of meaning, and a very relevant one at that, but they are also carriers of meaning. They not only accompany written language, but complement it and sometimes replace it; just think of the importance that images acquire in electronic hypertext (STORTO, 2011, p. 21).

Sometimes a single #moji is able to demonstrate or even express the state in which the sender is. This can be seen in the different responses to image 22, where by applying a single Emoji the user can make themselves understood, in responses such as "It's *cool, it's favourable"* or "on *top of the beef jerky*", which solely determine the current state of the sender.

4. 13SLEEPING FACE

IMAGE 23: Sleeping face

SOURCE: http://emojipedia.org/sleeping-face/

Face with eyes closed and a sleep symbol - *Zzz* - above the head. Usually used instead of the sleepy face to indicate a lot of sleep and drowsiness. The Emoji in image 23 is called *"Sleeping Face"*. There were 98 responses, 90 of which were similar to the original, and the dissimilarities are listed below.

Table 13: List of dissimilar results for the "S/eeping *Face"* Emoji:

Good evening
I never use
At last
How boring
When I'm tired

Source: Field research.

When the parties involved in the dialogue are already familiar with the use of

Emoji with the same connotation, even if the meaning applied is not original, this does not influence the dialogue. According to Storto (2011), the interactants in the conversational act, being familiar with these resources, use them without difficulty and with great variety, so that the conversation is established and there is no doubt.

4.14PERSON WITH HANDS TOGETHER

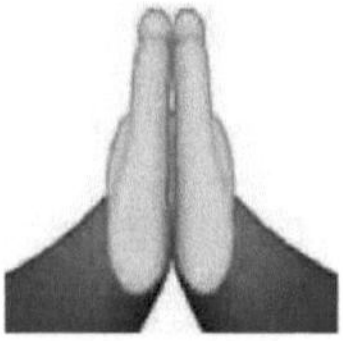

IMAGE 24: Person with hands together

SOURCE: http://emojipedia.org/person-with-folded-hands/

Two hands placed firmly together, meaning please or thank you in Japanese culture. Other common uses for this character include prayer/praying hands, or a high-five. Depicted in the image above, the Emoji is known as "Person *With Folded Hands"*, translating as "person with hands together". Of the 159 answers to this question, 151 were similar to the official meaning of the sign, with the main differences listed below.

Table 14: Main divergent answers for the sign "Person With Folded Hands":

Waiting
How nice
Peace
Thanks
Begging

Source: Field research.

Although Emojis have a formal meaning, this does not prevent them from being applied in a different way, for a different purpose. What's more, each culture can make its own sense of a particular sign. In the different responses to the Emoj i "Person *With Folded Hands*", among them "Peace" and "begging" can be considered correct, depending on the context in which it was applied.

In this respect, Storto (2011) emphasises that Emoji are not only made up of a signifier and a signified, but are also made up of meanings, which are attributed to them according to the virtual communicative context. This explains the amount of variation in meanings for the same Emoji, given that they are assigned according to the context to which a sign is contrasted.

4.15PERSON RAISING BOTH HANDS IN CELEBRATION

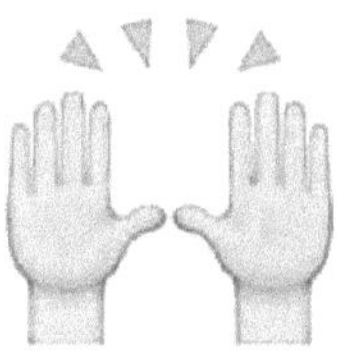

IMAGE 25: Person Raising Both Hands in Celebration

SOURCE: http://emojipedia.org/person-raising-both-hands-in-celebration/

Two hands raised in the air, celebrating success or another joyous event. Image 25 shows the Emoji officially called "Person *Raising Both Hands in Celebration"* or commonly known as "person raising *both* hands in celebration". Of the 199 responses to this question, 89 confirmed that they use Emoji for this purpose. The main differences are shown in the table below.

Chart 15: Main distinct responses to the Emoji "Person *Raising Both Hands in Celebration"*:

Confirmation
Stop
I'm here
We're together
Vibration

Source: Field research.

Even if there are variations for the same sign, this doesn't mean that communication will be distorted; after all, it is always necessary to analyse the way in which a particular Emoji has been applied in the discourse. Thus, Storto (2011) emphasises that through characteristics, the user interconnects information intuitively, associatively. The reader thus takes on an active role, being a co-author of the text at the same time.

The interpretation of the content of the speech also depends on the receiver of the message, so that both parties have the same understanding of the sign applied. In the answers in chart 15, such as "vibration" or "I'm here", understanding must be mutual, for sender and receiver, so that communication can take place smoothly.

4.16PERSON BOWING

IMAGE 26: A person bending over

SOURCE: http://emojipedia.org/person-bowing-deeply/

A person bowing deeply which is known as dogeza[5] in Japan. Used to express a sincere apology, or to ask for a big favour. This Emoji also looks a bit like a man doing push-ups, or lying down to have a massage.

Represented in the image above is the Emoji *"Peroon Bowing Deepiy*', or popularly known as "peoooa *oe curvando".* Of the 166 responses to this sign, only 4 assumed they were using the sign with its real meaning. Below is a list of the main dissimilar responses.

Chart 16: Main dissimilar responses to the "Person Bowing Deeply" Emoji:

Thoughtful
Little Angel
Burning neurons
Headache
Praying

Source: Field research.

It is necessary to analyse the context and the form of dialogue in order to

[5] https://en.wikipedia.org/wiki/Dogeza

interpret the meaning in which some Emojis are used. Given that in some cases Emojis can occupy or obtain several

different meanings. This can be seen in question 16, where only 4 answers were consistent with the real meaning of the sign, answers such as "thoughtful" or "praying" were quite frequent *IN* relation to this sign. Madureira and Souza (2015, p. 11) state that:

> [...] it is necessary to analyse the context in which the signs were used, in other words, what the other person meant when they chose that **Emoji** among so many others, so that the interpretation can be carried out coherently. Throughout this process, the mind is intensely exercised (MADUREIRA; SOUZA, 2015. p. 11).

A view with which the authors of this text are in full agreement.

4.17 NEW MOON WITH FACE

IMAGE 27: New Moon with Face

SOURCE: http://emojipedia.org/new-moon-with-face/

It's a new moon with a face, hiding in the shadows. Sometimes perceived as scary, it's actually a normal new moon with a face. Image 27 is officially called "New *Moon With Face"* or "new moon with a face" in popular parlance. Of the 179 answers for the meaning of this sign, only 26 answered with a meaning similar to the official one. The main answers with different meanings are listed below.

Chart 17: Main different meanings for the "New Moon With Face" Emoji:

Irony
When I don't agree with something or someone
Naughtiness
The evening promises
Watching

Source: Field research

Controversial emojis like the one illustrated in image 27 have meanings that vary according to age group, geographical region, social level, etc. Where the parties involved in the dialogue need to have the same understanding of the sign. With regard to this variation, Madureira and Souza (2015) emphasise that people need to be in the same social context to understand symbols in the same way. Interpretations are based on what the individual has experienced, on their cultural baggage.

It is therefore necessary for the parties to be synchronised on the same level in order to be able to communicate successfully. This explains the variants that exist for the same Emoji, as can be seen in the table above: while some users see the sign as having a sexual tone, others see it as a symbol of observation.

4.18 STRONG HEART

IMAGE 28: Strong Heart

SOURCE: http://emojipedia.org/heavy-black-heart/

A classic red heart, used to express love. Despite the name "Strong Heart". When used alone in a WhatsApp® message, this red heart Emoji becomes animated and pulsating. Illustrated in image 28, the "Heavy *Black Heart*" Emoji received 102 responses, 97 of which use the Emoji with its real meaning. The differences are shown below.

Chart 18: Existing divergences for the "Heavy Black Heart" Emoji:

Hallucinating
I don't use it
Waiting
It depends on the situation
Thanking someone

Source: Field research.

Emojis are intended to illustrate the image of the human face, demonstrating emotion in long-distance dialogue. According to Brito (2008, p. 5):

> These image signs help in digital communication by also expressing the affectivity of the interlocutors, since without affectivity, communication would only be mechanical. Therefore, as well as being instruments that facilitate communication, emojis are also signs that represent feelings and affectivity.

Even though an Emoji has a universal representation, it can be applied in countless situations. The answers in picture 18 show the variation in meaning for the same sign, even though it apparently has a universal meaning. Answers such as "thanking someone" or "hallucinating" are variations of the sign in image 18, but it can be seen that affectivity is still present in the discourse.

4.19 MALICIOUS FACE

IMAGE 29: Malicious Face

SOURCE: http://emojipedia.org/smirking-face/

A face with a mischievous smile, often used with a sexual or smug connotation. It should not be confused with the sullen face, which has similar eyes but a disgruntled mouth. Image 29 is officially called "Smzrhng *Face*[1] ', which roughly translates as "malicious smile". Faced with this question, 98 of the 201 answers to this question resemble those who use Emoji with this connotation. Here are the main differences:

Table 19: Main divergences for the **"Smirking Face" or** "Mischievous Smile" Emoji:

Indifferent
Undecided
Debauchery
Sad
Dull

Source: Field research.

Emojis can be applied to any type of dialogue and bring informality to virtual communication, making it more dynamic. According to Storto (2011), they are codes used by instant messaging users and can be part of informal conversations or not, with the function of making them more expressive. In the different responses to image 29, it can be seen that Emoji can also have variations, and make the sign have a more dynamic meaning, such as "debauchery" or "indifferent".

4.20 GRUMPY FACE

PICTURE 30: Grumpy face
SOURCE: http://emojipedia.org/unamused-face/

This is not a happy face, nor is it a face of sadness; it's more of a sullen look, one that is displeased. Used to express dissatisfaction or general disinterest. Represented in image 30, the Emoji called *"Uaamseed Fac^* or popularly known as "grumpy face". 201 answers were obtained for this question, 56 of which are similar to the official meaning. The main different answers are listed below.

Table 20: Top answers with different meanings for the "Uaamused *Face"* emoji:

Frowning
Angry
Bored
Fake
Off topic

Source: Field research.

With the variation in meaning attributed to the same Emoji and the misrepresentation that this variation can cause in communication, the answers in table 20 show that a greater understanding and analysis of the content of the message is needed to understand the intonation that a particular Emoji conveys in the dialogue. Madureira and Souza (2015) state that even with globalisation, virtual signs do not become a universal language because they are not understood in the same way. Therefore, it is necessary to universalise the meanings of Emojis, given that this variation can alter the meaning of the dialogue.

4.22 GENERAL DISCUSSION ASPECTS

This section seeks to discuss in a very specific way, after analysing the data obtained in the research, what meanings were attributed to Emojis in non-verbal communication within WhatsApp® and what were the approximations and divergences in the different concepts attributed to WhatsApp® Emojis.

Because they are digital signs, the Emojis in the WhatsApp® application have different meanings attributed to them. It was noted that these signs are widely used in communication mediated through WhatsApp® as a tool to make digital dialogue more dynamic and meaningful. They bring personality and practicality to communication.

In order for non-verbal communication to be interpreted correctly by all parties involved in the discourse, it needs to be universalised, so that there is no misrepresentation of meaning. With regard to the use of Emoji in digital discourse, through non-verbal communication, using these signs, it is necessary that the parties involved use the sign with the same connotation, so that communication takes place in a concise and coherent manner.

In the research carried out, it was observed that these digital signs cannot yet be considered universalised signs, as the meanings attributed to these Emojis are still quite varied and distinct from each other, with significant changes in the meanings attributed to the same sign in question. The similarity of Emojis to human faces, expressions and emotions means that, at a given moment in the discourse, the user identifies with the sign and applies it to their message. Therefore, each user has the capacity to interpret the image in different ways, making the meaning of the Emoji flexible in the context in which it is contrasted.

According to Fonte and Caiado (2014), visual language has its own syntax since its elements are organised to express coherent meanings. In this way, the relationship between text and image can ensure that even if the variation in meaning exists within the discourse, it is understood by the parties involved in the conversation.

Within this context, it can be said that the use of Emojis with different meanings occurs through the variation of meaning with which they are used. Therefore, each user's interpretation of a particular sign causes this variant to increase and thus create new meanings for a single Emoji.

According to Fonte and Caiado (2014), the way in which verbal language relates to non-verbal language contributes to the construction of meaning in dialogical interaction. The WhatsApp® application makes it possible to mix verbal and non-verbal language to construct meaning. In this way, the use of Emojis applied in a given discourse together with verbal language determines the meaning of the Emoji in the dialogue.

When analysing the results obtained in the survey, it was noticeable that the meanings attributed to the same sign vary. In this way, it can be seen that even though Emoji have characteristics similar to human faces and expressions, it is still possible to vary the meanings of this sign.

Among the results obtained in the survey, there were both similar and different concepts for the same sign. This is due to the variation in each user's knowledge and understanding of the world, as well as the culture to which they belong. There were cases in which a sign obtained answers that were totally similar to the real meaning, and there were cases in which the answers were totally distant from the literal meaning of the sign.

> [...] the sign has different social applications that provide different experiences, from the caves to the Emojis used in virtual communication. Therefore, icons are capable of propagating information regardless of the channel and time in which they are used (MADUREIRA; SOUZA, 2015 p. 13).

Based on this precept, it can be said that signs will always be in an infinite process of revolution and will hardly ever be universalised into a single meaning. However, this means that digital communication will always be this cycle of varied meanings and senses. Linguistics and linguistic signs are present in any context and the meanings attributed to these signs will inevitably vary.

CHAPTER 5

FINAL CONSIDERATIONS

Based on the assumptions raised, it can be concluded that the non-verbal language that occurs through the Emojis of the WhatsApp® application has been quite notorious in terms of the meaning attributed to these signs. Since the dawn of time, human beings have felt the need to communicate and make themselves understood, and through signs their communication has become increasingly adapted and easy to understand.

Human beings have always used signs to express themselves and make themselves understood through speech. With the revolution in instant messaging, these signs have also undergone major changes, up to and including the well-known Emojis in the WhatsApp® application. These, in turn, are not just decorative devices for discourse mediated through the app, but signs that carry meaning and complement distance communication. Emojis therefore play an important role in this context, as a single sign can be used to understand the meaning of a particular message.

The research showed that Emojis have different applications in terms of the different meanings attributed to the same sign. This is because the culture in which each user is inserted makes them attribute a different meaning to the sign, thus causing this multiple choice of application for the Emoji in question.

In view of this, it can be seen that Emojis, even though they have similar characteristics to human expressions, cannot yet be considered universal signs. However, the importance of these signs within digital discourse is indisputable. After all, in addition to making communication more attractive and playful, they carry the expressiveness that exists in personal communication, making discourse uncomplicated and natural.

It's a fact that Emojis have unique powers as linguistic resources capable of maintaining a conversation or ending it. Because the imposition of meaning or the construction of meaning is mutual between senders and receivers, but they can generate noise that disrupts communication. Today, these signs reflect the mode of communication of an era, perhaps strange to previous generations or those who don't use these resources.

Far from ending the contingencies of knowledge about digital signs (Emojis), this book seeks to stimulate future studies with the aim of exploring other trends in digital communication. Given that expectations about this universe are always growing and full of meaning.

REFERENCES

ALCURE, Lenira Ferraz. Verbal and non-verbal communication. 2 ed. Rio de Janeiro : Senac, 1996.

BORBA, Francisco. Introduction to linguistic studies. Campinas: Pontes, 1998.

BRITO, Audrey. The discourse of affectivity and the language of emoticons. Revista Eletrônica de Divulgação Científica em Língua Portuguesa, Linguística e Literatura, 2008.

BUENO, Amanda. Use of Messenger Applications in Conflict Resolution. Curitiba. INTERCOM. 2014.

CASTELLS, M. The network society. 8 ed. São Paulo: Ed. Paz e Terra, 2005.

CASTRO, Isa. Verbal and non-verbal language: teaching Portuguese. 2013.

CHAUÍ, Marilena. Invitation to Philosophy. São Paulo: Ática. 2000.

CORRAZE, J. Non-verbal communications. Rio de Janeiro, Zahar, 1982.

DUCROT, Oswald; TODOROV, Tzvetan. Encyclopaedic Dictionary of the Sciences of Language. São Paulo: Editora Perspectiva S.A., 1998.

FONTE, Renata; CAIADO, Roberta. Multimodal discursive practices on Whatsapp: a verb-visual analysis. 2014.

GOMES, Eduardo. Writing in human history. 2007. Available at: <http://dialogica.ufam.edu.br/PDF/no3/Eduardo_Aspectos_da_escrita_na_Historia_da_humanidade.pdf> Accessed on: 28 November 2016.

LARROSE Robert; STRAUBHAAR, Joseph D. Comunicação, mídia e tecnologia. São Paulo: Pioneer Thomson Learning, 2004.

LEMOS, A.; VALENTIM, J. Cyberculture and wireless network infrastructure in Brazil. Communication and Society. São Paulo, v.27, n.45, p.79-94, 2006

LÉVY, P. What is virtual? São Paulo: Editora 34, 1996.

LUFT, Celso Pedro. Modern Brazilian Grammar. São Paulo: Globo, 1994.

MADUREIRA, Gisela; SOUZA, Letícia. From Rock Painting to the Use of Symbols in the Exchange of Mobile Phone Instant Messages. Rio de Janeiro: INTERCOM, 2015.

MARTINO, L.C. The semiotic point of view. In: HOHLFELDT, A.; MARTINO, L. C; FRANÇA, V. (Orgs.). Communication theories: concepts, schools and trends. 9 ed. Petrópolis, Vozes, 2010.

MESQUITA, Rosa Maria. Non-Verbal Communication: Relevance in Professional Performance. Revista Paulista de Educação Física, São Paulo, v. 11, n. 2, p. 155-63, jul./dez. 1997.

MONTEIRO, Daniele. Instant Communicators: From the beginning to the present day. Article. 2011. Available at: <http://www.techtudo.com.br/artigos/noticia/2011/06/comunicadores- instantaneos-do-inicio-a-tempos-atuais.html>. Accessed on: 28 November 2015 at 15:45.

ORRICO, Alexandre. Are emojis racist? Online petition wants to include more diversity in the iPhone keyboard. Available at: http://blogdetec.blogfolha.uol.com.br/2013/09/05/os-emojis-sao-racistas- peticao-on-line-quer-incluir-mais-diversidade-no-teclado-do-iphone/. Accessed on: 13 October 2016.

RIBEIRO, Viviane. Cuneiform Writing. Available at: http://historiavivi.blogspot.com.br/2010/05/escrita-cuneiforme.html. Accessed on: 28 November 2015 at 14:56hrs.

SAUSSURE, Ferdinand de. Course in general linguistics. São Paulo: Cultrix Publishing House, 2006.

SOARES, Magda. Language and school: a social perspective. 16 ed. São Paulo: Ática, 1999.

STORTO, Letícia Jovelina. Emoticons: props for virtual conversations? ReVEL, v. 9,

n. 16, 2011.

VICENTE, Claudia. The New Mobile Communication Fever: WhatsApp. São Paulo. 2014.

ZACHARIAS J.J.M. Psicologia e informática: desenvolvimentos e progressos. São Paulo: Editora Casa do Psicólogo , 2005.

MIX
Papier aus verantwortungsvollen Quellen
Paper from responsible sources
FSC® C105338

Printed by Books on Demand GmbH, Norderstedt / Germany